I WAS MORE AMERICAN
THAN THE AMERICANS

T0083495

I Was
More American
than the Americans

Sylvère Lotringer
in Conversation with
Donatien Grau

Diaphanes

Some ten years ago, I first visited Sylvère Lotringer. I was a young scholar from France and worked mostly on nineteenth- and twentieth-century literary history. I was travelling to Los Angeles to meet Paul McCarthy, and visiting Sylvère felt like one of the worlds L.A. could open up for me. I had been familiar with Sylvère's work as a bridge between so-called "French Theory"—whose hippest, boldest, most artistic moves he manifested and often made happen—and the places where it revealed itself, from New York to L.A. on to the deserts of New Mexico. I was also familiar with Sylvère's advocacy for Pierre Guyotat, the legendary author and artist I was beginning to be close to.

I remember Sylvère sat in the shade under the Californian sun. At first, he seemed to feel he was welcoming quite a boring scholar: he told me about Columbia, about Antoine Compagnon's choice to study literary history. We barely spoke about Semiotext(e). As years passed and I spent more and more time in L.A., I went to see him again, and again. It wasn't until 2014 that we began a clear process of interviews. The very first was for *Purple*: Olivier Zahm, the editor, had founded his magazine in loving memory of what Semiotext(e) was throughout the 70s and 80s. We worked on this interview relentlessly, and after it was done and published, I felt— and it seems Sylvère felt as well—that we needed more: that he and I had so much to say to each other. I then offered to Sylvère that we carry on with these conversations. And that is what we have been doing, for the last five years: and that is what you will read.

The first conversation was *Purple*'s, and it is an overview of Sylvère's life. Sylvère has done many interviews on Semiotext(e). He himself is a fantastic interviewer, and somewhere in his archives—I haven't kept it—there is a conversation where he interviews me. Maybe it was my work on how Proust absorbed Sainte-Beuve, but I felt that a part was missing in Sylvère's discussions: an overview of him, his friendships, his teaching, some aspects that were dear to his heart. That is also what this book is. Some conversations we held in private, he and I, at his house. Two of them we held in public: the first took place at The Box, Mara McCarthy's space, where I've been organizing a series of discussions titled "The Anatomy of Subversion." Sylvère was in the first round. The second was part of a panel on Pierre Guyotat, on the occasion of his and Christoph von Weyhe's exhibition at the same space. One of the greatest compliments I've been paid was when Sylvère told me, after the first round, "This is Semiotext(e), just somewhere else." This is etched in my mind, as a motto, and a calling.

Along the way, thanks to Sylvère, I got to meet Iris Klein and spend time with Noura Wedell, Hedi El Kholti, and Chris Kraus, and to witness admiringly what they have been doing with Semiotext(e), alongside Sylvère. With these conversations, my aim was simply to give a feeling of what an extraordinary person Sylvère is. They're just snippets into his being. But they are of such richness. Thank you Sylvère, for allowing me to be your conversation partner; thank you Hedi, for being such a friend; thank you Iris, for all your wisdom; and thank you Pierre, as always.

Donatien Grau

Beginnings

DONATIEN GRAU: You are widely credited with having introduced French Theory in America in the 1980s and permanently changing the face of the art world. It didn't happen overnight.

SYLVÈRE LOTRINGER: It wasn't planned, no one seemed to be interested in it. Publishers found the theories too specialized and downtown artists disliked intellectuals intensely, probably because they were intellectuals themselves. French theorists were fascinated by New York but didn't know much about it. I didn't know so much about it either, but I realized what was there. I just happened to be at the right time at the right place. I saw what could be done. Things could have turned out differently.

DG: You came from a Jewish Polish family from Warsaw, and you were in hiding during the Second World War. Later on, still a child, you became part of a radical Zionist group. It seems to me that this experience—the feeling of belonging to a persecuted minority and the production of a community—has had a big impact on your life.

SL: It shaped my life. I trained myself to surmount any situation. My parents moved to Israel in 1949 to join close relatives who had emigrated to Palestine in the early 1930s. We had had such a hard time in France during the war that they said: why don't you come to Israel? So we emigrated to Israel when I was ten. The state hardly existed. I stayed there for about a year and a half. It was the Wild West. I collected tortoises and snakeskins. I went to school and learned Hebrew. And then my family couldn't find a way of staying there. There was no infrastructure. There was no economy. On top of that, their job was to make furs: that wasn't exactly the country to do it in, although there was a little snow in Jerusalem that year. They couldn't find an apartment. They said, "Look, we were dispersed during the war, we are not going to be dispersed now in Israel. Let's go back to Paris." And so we did.

DG: Strangely enough, they took you to a militant Zionist group as soon as you returned.

SL: They already belonged to it in Warsaw. The movement, as we called it, was just being reborn in Paris after the war along the lines of the Soviet youth. I was eleven, the youngest and the only one at the time, with my sister, to have been to Israel. It became mythical, even for me. The movement encouraged us to see it that way. We never talked about Arabs living there, except for friendly Druzes who invited you under their tents. The idea that another people could have belonged there before we did, and had been chased away in 1948 to make room for us, never crossed our minds. We had just been through hell and the *Exodus* ship was only three years before. The movement was radical, but it was Zionist all the same. Its goal was to take us away from our petit bourgeois background. Our goal was to create Bar Am, a new kibbutz at the border with Lebanon. It is still there. The kibbutz movement was ascendant then. We would share everything, clothes, books, work, and create a new kind of humanity, less competitive and individualistic. Socialism was a reality. We were the first generation to survive the genocide and we had few examples to follow. We hardly talked about the recent past, except to exalt the Warsaw Ghetto Insurrection and compare it to the heroic resistance of the Maccabees. We were taught about dialectical materialism, and celebrated Jewish festivals. We were told about sexuality too, embarrassingly. Our "mentors" were hardly older than we were. The sexes were kept separate, and everyone groped in the dark.

I became one of the leaders of this movement in France, but I realized that they were all afraid that, if I stayed too long in France, I would get too interested in university. I had to make a choice. Either I was going to the kibbutz and working the land or I wanted to start my studies. I didn't see that there was a contradiction between the two. But people did see it that way. I was interested in art. My teacher sent me to a night school on rue Lepic, behind the Sacré-Coeur—I saw my first nude models there—and I painted frescoes on the walls of our "local" (the meeting place of the movement). I also made a mimeographed journal for the movement—my first magazine—in which I attacked Jean-Paul Sartre for being too bourgeois.

DG: You also participated in Georges Perec's *La Ligne générale* in 1959–1960.

SL: Roger Kleman, Perec's right hand, was in my class at the Lycée Jacques Decourt, and we competed for prizes. He was the one who recruited me. The circle met on rue de Trévise, just one block from my parents', and everyone was mostly Jewish. Henri Lefebvre, the Marxist philosopher, mentioned *La Ligne générale* (after Sergei Eisenstein) in the same breath as the Situationist International, praising our brand of revolutionary romanticism, but I only met him much later, when I was at the Sorbonne and asked him to write an essay on the "possible" for the student journal.

In 1958, sitting for my *baccalauréat*, the dissertation topic for the writing portion was: "What is an ideal?" And of course, very few people had any sort of idea about ideals. But for me, it was not a philosophical problem. It was a very pragmatic one. I must have been so unproblematic about it that they flagged me in the first session—the June session. I had to spend the summer with my parents in Nice, studying Jean-Paul Sartre again. I got more into it this time over. The pressure of the movement was getting intense. Some twenty-five of us coming from everywhere, all of the same age, met to work in an experimental farm in the South of

France and develop strong bonds in preparation for our departure to Israel. It was a disturbing experience.

We had committed to leave France in the coming months against the wishes of our families. (I learned masonry to have a skill to fall back on). Raised communally, we were suddenly being asked to make our "self-criticism," Soviet style, in front of everyone else. We felt pretty raw. Each evening after a lengthy "confession," we scattered away by twos, each sex apart, along the road that bordered the farm. Until then we had lived like brothers and sisters and we were shocked to have to look at each other differently. It felt really incestuous. One night, outside, an incoming car skidded and hit a comrade. He was killed on the spot. We were all crying. Our confessions, this death, it was just all too much.

I had come to the farm late because of my exam. Now it was clear that I felt tempted to stay a bit longer, maybe enroll at the Sorbonne. The movement refused. As a compromise, they offered me to take charge of the movement in Metz, which had no university. The message was clear.

DG: Is that when you met Georges Lapassade?

SL: He was the philosopher who had interrogated me for the orals. He asked me what dreaming about a chimney meant. [*Laughs*] He noticed my confusion and gave me his phone number. I spoke to him and asked, "What should I do?" And he said, "Why don't you resign?" I said, "Resign?" The idea had never crossed my mind. Does one resign from one's parents? I typed the letter all the same, but the movement knew, of course, that it could only have come from someone outside. There was no way back.

Lapassade was putting together a small group that met twice a week at the École Normale Supérieure on rue d'Ulm to test Moreno's group dynamics. He invited me to join in with three other students from the JC [Communist Youth] who obviously believed in an ideal as well. They were on the student committee of the Sorbonne and were looking for a president whose political position wouldn't be a problem. I was the perfect candidate. I came from nowhere.

The situation in France was catastrophic and I got deeply involved in it. For two years I was in charge of *Paris-Lettres*, the Sorbonne's newspaper, and reported on tortures. I maintained contact with democratic and Algerian students opposing right-wing rebels in Algiers. It wasn't what I expected to do at the Sorbonne, but I had little choice. The Algerian War of Independence was engulfing everything. In 1954 the Front de Libération Nationale (FLN) had launched armed revolts throughout Algeria. It was met with harsh repression, entire villages displaced or eradicated, villagers tortured and executed summarily. The conflict bled into the metropolis. We were demonstrating in the street every day. One and a half million conscripts were sent to Algeria and paratroopers were ready to be parachuted over Paris.

DG: Didn't you start another magazine at the time?

SL: Yes. It was called *L'Etrave* [Spur] and I created it in 1960 with some friends from the Sorbonne, like Bertrand Tavernier and Luc Boltanski. For a few years it remained attached to the Sorbonne, then it was turned into an independent journal with co-editor Nicole Chardaire. Paradoxically, a rich cultural production had emerged in Paris from Ionesco and Beckett to Alain Robbe-Grillet and Marguerite Duras. We didn't see any contradiction between these writers' experimental outlook and their political engagement. Needless to say, I only had little time to study, although I had to pass my exams each year in order to defer conscription. My professors at the Sorbonne would have let me through anyway, but I was there to acquire a culture, and in 1961 I took a year off to teach French in a high school in Edinburgh. I prepared my exams on my own and I passed effortlessly. That year was a crucial year for me. For the first time I was alone, read enormously and started writing. It also gave me the idea that I could teach abroad. I wanted to learn more about the world.

DG: In 1959, Olivier Burgelin, who directed the Maison des Lettres on rue Férou, a cultural center for Sorbonne students, had approached you to organize events there.

SL: It got me closer to the intellectual scene. I first met Roland Barthes, who was living nearby, in 1959 when Burgelin invited him to give a lecture on "Language and Clothes" and later became his assistant at the Collège de France. Literary criticism was thriving and I set up conferences on the Nouvelle Critique, with phenomenologist writers like Gaston Bachelard, Georges Poulet, Jean Starobinski, and Jean-Pierre Richard. I also invited Nouveau Roman writers—Claude Simon, Marguerite Duras, Robbe-Grillet—and sociologists Lucien Goldmann, Jean Duvignaud. I also wrote articles in *Combat* directed by Albert Camus under an alias (Lorger), and in *Les Lettres Françaises*, a literary magazine sponsored by the Communist Party and directed by liberal Surrealist poet Louis Aragon. For a number of years I freelanced for it regularly, reporting on the literary scene in England. I published special issues on Virginia Woolf, James Joyce, Brendan Behan, Dickens, etc. In 1964, for the celebration of Shakespeare's birthday, I attended all his plays in England, and Picasso made a drawing for the magazine.

In 1960 I did a long interview with Nathalie Sarraute in *L'Etrave* which introduced me to Virginia Woolf, whose work was hardly known in France at the time. Although I was a French major, I decided to write my dissertation on her novels. I was turned down as a non-specialist both by the English and the French departments at the Sorbonne, so instead I asked Lucien Goldmann and Roland Barthes, both "structuralists" whom I knew well, to direct my dissertation at the École Pratique des Hautes Études. It was the most exciting place intellectually in Paris, and I got involved with semiotics as it was quickly reshaping all the human sciences. The journal that I would put together in New York in 1973, *Semiotext(e)*, dealt with semiotics.

By 1962, I had run out of degrees to postpone the draft and applied for a teaching job in Iowa with the idea of dropping out of sight if the war hadn't stopped. (I owed the war my academic career). Fortunately, I didn't have to make a life-time decision. In the spring of that year, de Gaulle signed the Evian Accords with the FLN and I immediately applied to be sent as a "coopérant" [a Peace Corps Volunteer] at a university in Eastern Turkey. It was there on the high plateaus bordering Iran that I completed my dissertation.

DG: Can you tell me about the beginning of your teaching career abroad?

SL: I wanted to be as far as possible from France in order to end up being close. I had an MA. So with this, you couldn't do anything in France. It was like having nothing. So I was working for newspapers. I was working for French television. And I thought I would go on doing that. Then after a while I realized that it was like having compartments in my brain. Every week, I was reading a whole book to immediately write an account, a review of it, etc. But it was full of holes. And I thought that if I were a teacher, I would have more time to read, more time to be in touch with the culture. So that's what I did. I decided I was going to leave France. But the idea was that I was going to come back. Goldmann gave me some openings: I could have gone to teach in Chicago, but it was Vietnam. I didn't want to go to the United States. It was like Sartre.

So I went to Australia. In 1968, I was in Australia, and I was the only one to be a rebel there in front of my class. I was married with a French woman at the time, from the Communist Party, and then after a year and a half in Australia, I thought: this is impossible. You can't live in that country, because the salaries were very low, and the tickets to go back to France very high. And I met Italians who were crying because they would never be able to go back to Italy. So I decided after a year and a half that I would try and get closer to France. But I had to reimburse all the investment that Australia had made in my being an immigrant, because I hadn't been there for three years. If you really stay for three years, they wipe it out. But I left after a year and a half. So I had to repay them. So in order to repay them I looked for a job in the United States for a year. And it was very easy to find jobs then. I had six offers from Harvard, Yale, Columbia, and such places. It was Swarthmore we accepted. It was early 1969. The spring of 1969 was Kent State. And so the whole campus erupted. Everyone went on strike. Students didn't come to classes. They basically closed the college and were dedicated to the revolution full time. There was the idea that Philadelphia, which was pretty close, was in revolution, that the people would come from there. And so we reinvented revolution, but in such a beautiful landscape. Swarthmore is one of the most exquisite and rich colleges in the country. The value of having taught at Swarthmore was far superior to that of teaching at Columbia. The people who were at Swarthmore were mostly from very elite families.

But they were very radical, of course. That's the thing that happens everywhere. The most radical are almost always the most privileged—the ones who have the culture. My parents have no special culture. My mother had some pharmacy training in Poland, but my father had no training whatsoever. He trained to do furs because the family didn't want to let them go if they didn't have a job.

A few weeks after the college went on strike, news came that Philadelphia was not on fire. It was very easy to go with a train, twenty minutes by train, to check. And no one had done so until then. After a while, the administration said, well, you know, we think it's great that you're going out and making yourself available for society, but those who don't want to do that can pass their exams. So very fast, after two or three weeks, everyone took the exam. By the fall, everyone was back to normal, except that the contract of a colleague of mine wasn't renewed, and mine was renewable by year, so they didn't renew it either. So at that point, I had to leave Swarthmore, and I wanted to go back to France, but I was offered a job in Cleveland, Ohio, and I liked the guy who invited me to go there, so I said, okay, I'll go to Cleveland. So I was in Cleveland for two years. And after two years, I was getting really fed up with the Midwest, which is flat, flat, flat: flat landscape, flat mind. So I went to Columbia, back to number one. They were looking for someone, and I had published a lot. At the same time, my head of department in Cleveland said, "Well, Sylvère, if you don't want to teach a class in French language, I'm sorry but there are lots of

Americans who could do that." And at that time, exactly at that time, I got an offer from Columbia, so I said: "Fuck you." Then I left with a royal chariot.

DG: And then you were in a real city. You were in New York, and you were closer to France than you had been for a few years.

SL: I arrived in 1972. I had already spent summers there working in the collection of the New York Public Library, because they had manuscripts of Virginia Woolf, T. S. Eliot, etc. I was actually getting more interested in English and American literature than in French. But of course I was in a French department, and I taught mostly French writers. I was pleased to come to New York. The chair hired me because I was a good structuralist. For the first year I was at Columbia, I discovered the world of Columbia. And it took me two years to discover downtown. Downtown and uptown had no connection whatsoever. Columbia had its problems, with Harlem close by: it was very dangerous, and you never went out much at night, at the time.

One year after I arrived at Columbia, I decided to go to France. One of the reasons they had hired me at Columbia was the fact that I had organized summer schools in France for the various universities where I was teaching. I chose the place. I chose the teachers. And then we had students coming from not just Columbia, but other places. While I was in France, I invited people to teach who could help me compensate for the four years, or five years I hadn't been in France. I was one train late, you see? When I left France, you know, Barthes, the Nouvelle Critique, that was really what the intellectual scene was about. What came out next was very different: 1967 is Derrida's *Of Grammatology*. 1972 is *Anti-Oedipus*. So I arrived in a context that was fairly different from the one I expected. At the beginning, I invited formalists, but I became aware that there were other things happening in France, and at Columbia the chair, Riffaterre, had created a group of semioticians whom we trained in a structural approach to literature. But the group was having a problem with Riffaterre, because he was the one who trained them. They were at the stage where they were trying to take their distance from him. And here I come. Of course, I was the only one from the staff, and I started working with the little group. We were hovering between Guattari, Kristeva, Lévi-Strauss. We were also Althusserian, and we admired Bachelard. So we met and discussed all this. It was pretty intense. And then when I came back to France to teach the summer school, I discovered that I could take them to the chateau at Cerisy. So I resumed contact with people I knew from the Nouvelle Critique and the Nouveau Roman. There were a lot of people I didn't know. So I hired them and took their classes: Todorov, Denis Hollier, Catherine Clément, Jean-Louis Schefer, Guattari, of course, Serge Leclaire. A good sample of what was happening at the time. The first one who taught there was Guattari: I got very interested and, suddenly, I rediscovered politics. I was confronted with something that I didn't know before. Immediately, I realized that I could invite whoever I wanted. There were no American students in France at the time. So my group of twenty Americans met people who had never seen an American student before. They were curious. Since Guattari was teaching at Reid Hall, Deleuze made an impromptu visit, and he came and told us about the fact that philosophy is there to intimidate young men. Of course, I didn't believe a word, but it gave me a certain idea of how to teach Deleuze. And then Lacan came by, because he had heard about this place where Guattari and Deleuze were coming. So he came and flirted with my students with a cigar. Basically, it was a center of attraction, because it was the first kind of that extension of America in France. And so, even though I was teaching in the French department, I was in charge of teaching French literature and human sciences.

By then, I had developed a personal friendship with Felix and decided to take a leave of absence from Columbia to be with him and his group at the Laborde clinic, near Tours. In the summer of 1974, before I left Paris, I had the idea of bringing to New York the theorists who interested me most, because they were the most politically oriented. Together with John Rajchman, a graduate student in Philosophy at Columbia, who was on leave as well in Paris, we put together a conference in New York whose purpose was to present "post-structuralist" philosophy to the United States. In November 1975, an audience of some two thousand people was exposed for three days to a bombardment of concepts, to which they reacted sometimes with enthusiasm, often with anger and frustration. The "Schizo-Culture" conference, as it was called, turned out to be a major intellectual landmark and anticipated the way French Theory would sweep over America for the next decades.

DG: What became *Semiotext(e)* was coming out of formalism, coming out of semiotics itself, in a combination of strange ways of life, philosophy, psychoanalysis, politics. How did that crystallize?

SL: Well, it was happening in France. You know, philosophy, psychoanalysis, sociology, all this work goes together. And that is exactly what I had done at the Maison des Lettres. So I just found myself having recreated La Maison des Lettres on my own. The logic was the same: there was again a group, a group at Columbia. We were all kind of on the left. We didn't accept the tyranny of linguistics.

All the students I founded *Semiotext(e)* with were graduate students: they were finishing their dissertations, or were about to finish their dissertations. So after two years, they were looking for jobs all over the country. So when I came back, the little group that we had put together was half gone. We had to change it and restructure it. And that led to the magazine. When we created it, I went to a few publishers, and I told them: look, I know all these interesting people in France. If you manage the magazine the way magazines are managed by presses in France, then I will tell you who to publish. And they had a look at some of the texts. They said, "No. It will interest a handful of intellectuals, specialists." So we didn't have a choice: we created a magazine.

The inaugural issue was mimeographed. I went to Mexico at the time for a month, and the issue was ready to be finished. And we collated, going around the table. Everyone would make the book and take a page and go around. That was also very collective. Someone in the group kidnapped the magazine before the magazine was published. So before it happened, I already had group problems. Since we were looking for a title, I said, well, it's semio, but it's text. So Semiotext(e). No one understood what it was about, of course. Jack Smith once told me that the title was so disgusting: "Why did you choose a title like that?" The title is really what thinking is about.

The way I saw it was that we had a group, but according to my way, the chief is not the important one in the group. He is the one who doesn't want to be chief, but he doesn't have a choice, because to be chief, you have to divest yourself of everything you own. And I always thought a group was like that. The chief is a mediator. He creates good vibes and makes choices. But I'm not constantly on top of them. And so the group I had in New York just made me think more about groups. I realized that to be a group without a leader in America is impossible. Everyone is so self-centered, so eager to get recognition. What happened right after the beginning was a warning that I had to make sure that the group kept being collective, not a group of people who'd be competing. I never liked competing. See, I'm very un-American. So I decided that I would pay attention to the magazine, and always give each issue of the magazine to a different person. And they chose who they were working with. So it was democratic, but in fact, I made the major choices. Because someone has to do it. And if there isn't someone to push people, nothing is going to happen. So I got the idea at that time that yes, I could have a group, but I was working with friends. I was not working with people who were not my equals.

DG: *Semiotext(e)*, as a journal, was a platform that brought together artists and thinkers, which was very unusual at the time.

SL: I didn't know anything about art. In France, I would go to the Louvre. I was very good at drawing, so I took classes, but I had no sense of what art is. When I arrived in New York, I had no idea about art. So I was very open. And since my relation with my colleagues soured very fast, I was looking for some more interesting places. And there were lots of parties in New York. Actually, most of them were with South Americans, so I thought that the only people in New York were South American. New York is fragmented. You could get into a French community, the Spanish community, the English community.

I met interesting people along the way. I was going to parties a lot, because I was on my own. I broke up with my girlfriend. I was alone and was just meeting people.

DG: But how does a professor at Columbia go downtown and get to meet John Cage, Merce Cunningham, William Burroughs? How did that happen?

SL: William Burroughs I knew before I left. I heard of William Burroughs when I was in front of the Bibliothèque Sainte-Geneviève. When I arrived, I was looking for some sort of equivalent to Deleuze, Guattari, Foucault, Lacan. I was looking for a cultural context. I had no context. At the university, which is the only context I had, you have of course excellent specialists, but everyone is in their little department, in their little career, in their little values, etc. So I just was looking for something else. I didn't know it would be the art world. But then New York at that time was very easygoing. You had the liaisons. You have, you know, people who are sleeping with each other a lot, going to parties. There was a whole downtown culture. It was just pretty promiscuous. There were no rules, no regulations. You know, you do what you want. You want to love people, you want to make love, it doesn't matter. You know, things can happen. And at all these parties I went to, I met some people who were interesting. It so happened that they were artists. Academics were not going to these parties. They were all artists.

DG: How did you get to go to these parties? How did you hear about them?

SL: I think the first one was a South American I met, and she took me to a number of parties with people from Peru, from Central America. But then I met other people, and then I would just say, "Maybe that could be interesting for the group." I met Pat Steir—she was the only one my age in the group—and her boyfriend for a long time was Sol LeWitt. She was part of the old SoHo, and she knew everyone: Philip Glass, Richard Serra. They were just friends. So while I was still at Columbia, and I was with the group, I was becoming more and more a downtown person. When I had the magazine, I said, okay. Well maybe I'll do the same as I did before, which is: I'm going to interview these people. That way, I'm going to learn about them. I like theory, but theory connected to something. I'm not a pure theorist or philosopher. I learned art with artists.

DG: And who were the artists you were most interested in?

SL: Well, I was always interested, because I didn't make choices. There was post-minimal, and there were the conceptual artists. I was willing to accept anything, because I didn't have any pre-conceived idea of what art should be. Look at what all the French philosophers wrote about art: it was always on classical art. They had no idea what was going on. Deleuze quotes Patti Smith, but because he came to the States for the Schizo-Culture convention, and then met Smith and Allen Ginsberg. Most of the people in the group had no idea what I was talking about. But it was something that no one knew. It was a very good incentive. So they started reading Lacan. And I had the same idea. The idea was to do things with downtown people.

The magazine was not the only thing I was doing. I had three or four friends who were dealing with different issues of the magazine. In the meantime, since I met all these interesting people, I invited them to come and work for the group, and if they were up for it, that was great for me. I had some idea of what they were doing, but also they belonged to a context that I realized was much more interesting than academe. So I had the most diverse people, people who didn't even like each other.

I put together an issue on Nietzsche, because I realized that Nietzsche was not known in this country. He was known as someone who writes nice little stories for kids. It was too romantic. And this was associated with a total misrepresentation of Nietzsche: the others who knew about Nietzsche thought that he was a Nazi. So I thought, let's clear the slate, and let's have a special issue on Nietzsche. The first book I published with Semiotext(e) was not a French book. It was an American book. It was the book by Cage and the musicologist Daniel Charles called *For the Birds*. I read the book, and I said, "Wow, this is putting together Zen Buddhism and Nietzsche." When I read this book—it was a book of interviews—I realized: here is the connection. He's American, but he works in music, and the music is based on Nietzsche, and all sorts of these Eastern philosophies. And I realized, reading Deleuze and

Guattari, what many people notice, it's much more connected to Eastern philosophy than to the philosophy they developed in Europe. So I went to see Cage, and I said, "Well, I'm doing an issue on Nietzsche. Would you like to contribute to it?" So he said yes. He sent me a piece. But before I left, he said, "You're French." I said, "Yes." He said, "Do you play chess?" I knew enough to know that Cage played chess with Marcel Duchamp, so I said, "Yes, yes, of course I play." So: "We should play one of these days." But I was really afraid of coming back. So I didn't call him back. And after a few weeks, he called me, and he said, "When are we playing chess?"

DG: At that time you brought together philosophy, music, dance, art. Can you tell me about those interactions?

SL: First of all, Americans heard about semiotics. Artists were interested in semiotics, communication. But they didn't know what it meant. One of the reasons so many people came to the Schizo-Culture conference was that a friend at the *Village Voice*, friend of friends, put up an ad for Semiotext(e), and he said it's a Semiotext(e) event about semiotics. So we got all the people coming, all the artists. Artists always want to know, and know about things before the others. They had heard about semiotics, but they didn't know what it was. So a lot of people came just for that reason. The others, you know, for political, philosophical reasons. But yes, there was no event like that, blending music, dance, art, philosophy.

My idea was that the magazine had a very limited audience. I realized that my audience was the people we knew. When we printed three or four hundred copies, they were gone in two weeks. I understood that the magazine needed to reach more people. In the 70s, there were very few artists. But at the same time there were very few people other than artists. It was a time when the art world was changing from inside and from outside. From outside, it was the Italian and German neo-expressionists coming to conquer New York between 80 and 82, and then the neo-conceptualists reacting and re-establishing the balance for the Americans.

It was just the end of the 70s. In the 1970s, all the artists were doing other things: Sol LeWitt was sponsoring Kathy Acker because she had no money. It was a small community. Everyone knew each other and each other's work. So I always learned about someone through someone else. But constantly, the people who were the most interesting turned out to be these artists. That's why I decided to meet them, not on the chance occasion. I went to see Phil Glass, who's a friend of my friend Pat Steir. And she says, "Go and see Phil Glass. He's a very good musician." No one knew Phil Glass at the time, really. And Steve Reich, and these people. They were known in an artistic circle, but not outside. So I talked to them, and Phil Glass said, "Oh, but you should know Jack Smith." I said, "Who is Jack Smith?" He'd say, "If you want to know about the American surrealists, go and see Jack Smith." So I went to see Jack Smith, and it turned out to be something completely different.

He's the first artist who told me, "Look, you're interested in the art, I can tell."

I started getting to know people who were all kind of artists or weirdos. Downtown was full of them. There were the club people I was meeting in clubs. Along the way I met Stefan Eins, and Diego Cortez, who was not a Latino but took the name of a Latino to get a grant from a university. He was Mr. Punk. King downtown. He was pre-punk: the Ramones had already started in the States before they went on tour in London. Diego had a finger in every pie. He was manager of the real hardcore punk. He was doing graffiti with kids' drawings. I moved in with him, and we had a big loft in the Fashion District. I was going out with him to the Mudd Club, or to Max's Kansas City, and not only would bouncers not check him out, but they were unfolding the red carpet. It turns out that Diego was an artist who was afraid of showing his own art, so he was using the art of others, even stealing the art of others.

DG: How did you engage with culture? You had done the Schizo-Culture conference. It was not the time of counterculture anymore. You said that, even if your magazine was going to be sold to three people, it was being done for 200 million.

SL: The work I did was not a cultural work. It was the idea that I could live with nothing, and I could live with no one. It was paradoxical. Of course I lived with a group constantly. But the idea was that I had to be ready. It was a personal experience much more than a cultural one.

After we published one or two of the really consistent issues, people paid attention. I wanted to have an issue on nomadism. But I wasn't sure that we weren't more nomadic in New York than we were in the desert. So I went to the desert, and I spent nearly two weeks in the desert with the Tamacheck. I thought I would do something with that, but in fact at that time it was kind of getting late. I didn't want to make another issue of the magazine. So I asked a group of people to do it. And then they made an issue of *Semiotext(e)* that was exactly the reverse of what we do. We usually had four or five hundred pages. They made something that was 120. We had very functionalist aesthetics for the layout, and they had it very aestheticized. So after a while, I said: you're free to do what you want. I don't want to influence you. So do it. And what I didn't realize was that every time a group gets together, it becomes a group because they become antagonistic. So after a while, they developed an antagonism towards me. And when they finished the mockup of the magazine, they came and gave it to me, and I wasn't exactly pleased. I told them: you made the magazine for people in the East Village, but in order to publish issues of *Semiotext(e)*, I have to aim at 200 million Americans, and then a thousand, two thousand readers would be possible. The "Oasis" issue was so invisible that no one saw it. It's the only magazine that never sold.

French Theory was something that Americans, and artists in particular, didn't know. So *Semiotext(e)* became very important. Most people started reading it because it circulated, because it did circulate. And some of them took extreme measures. There were some artists who stopped making art because they had to read Saussure before. Michael Horowitz, who was also working with *Semiotext(e)*, had a big Lacan under his arm when he was teaching his classes. And I said, I don't know why people are afraid of me. It's snobbery in a good and bad way: in America, they always want to be first, but they are very open to embracing things, which is exactly the reverse of what was happening in France. In France, culture is for the elite. Culture is something separate.

In New York, I was kind of lost, but I discovered that to be on your own is such an incredible experience. I was just like anyone else. I did not have to know everything Foucault was writing on to be able to understand his work. It was something totally new for me. I could start from scratch. The idea is always: when you don't live in your country, then you create a floating island. That's how you can survive. I realized very early on that if I had to survive in American culture, where I feel so different from them, I had to create a kind of puzzle of people, who created a context for the culture, with the culture that existed.

DG: Now Semiotext(e) is a bit of a mythical thing in American intellectual and artistic history. What do you think you've achieved with Semiotext(e)?

SL: Bad things. The worst is that, from the very beginning, they misread it. People didn't read the magazine. They were dancing with the magazine. All these clubs that we were going to, these were our readers. The issues often had themes, the theme of the night. When we were publishing a book, I would come up with a theme, and then people were coming to clubs for Semiotext(e). The fact that we'd been making all these events was maybe different from any other magazine, because we were already a cultural magazine. We created events. We published artists. But what was important for me is the fact that whatever I did, I didn't want to belong anywhere. That's why I wanted to reach the culture at large, and not be an academic, not be an artist, not be a filmmaker, not be one thing. Same thing for my career: I published all the chapters that could have ended up in my book on the theory of the novel. Each was a different century, so that I could never be cornered and put somewhere. Basically, I always wanted to escape. When you escape, you just go someplace you don't know in advance. And I was going some other place. I was always attracted to the other place. I had to learn something along the way. It's not heroic. Culture was not something I had. Culture is something I built. And it was easier to build a culture in the States where nothing is closed. I had holes everywhere. But holes aren't so bad, because you can fill them in any way it happens. It happened along the way. But no one could tell that I was a fake.

DG: And did you have a feeling at that time in New York that there was a thing like an avant-garde?

SL: We didn't call it a counterculture anymore, because that was the 1960s. For us, it was more like the last of the avant-garde. In France, an avant-garde is a literary avant-garde—and painting, because they have to live off something. Here, the idea that the avant-garde was a group of guys simply didn't work. So you have all sorts of people, and they all kind of went to each other's events. Dancers were not just dancers. At the time, it was a community where they were the very, very informal participants in the arts scene.

The avant-garde to me was more the rock avant-garde. It was the Rolling Stones and all the other bands. The punk milieu was a first for me. And punk was not political: they were against politics. But they were very much into music, into popular music. So I got involved in both right away. I never heard rock before I arrived in New York. I never smoked dope. I think that that's what made something possible: I don't have a preconceived idea of what should exist and what shouldn't exist. I just followed what interested me. And it happened. It happened to be the time to do it. Pat Steir and her friends were part of the old art world. And the old art world had nothing to do with the punks. It's only at a certain date, when there was a turn from neo-expressionism to neo-conceptualism, that the art world started feeling a bit threatened by what was happening in the punk scene. I saw the first artists going secretly to their first punk concert in the East Village. And they were hiding: Richard Serra and Vito Acconci. There was a *relève de la garde*. Punk and popular culture were taking over from the classical, artistic avant-garde. You know, they were making paintings. There was a floating moment, which is when we started publishing the books. Neo-expressionism brought painting back to New York: they brought something that could be sold. At the time, prior to that, the little art world could exist on its own: there were three or four galleries, which did not sell anything. And then all that changed.

Semiotext(e) was not that known, but known enough to be part of that. I was very tolerant. I liked going to clubs and I liked having a joint here and there and trying everything I could try. But I also liked the neo-conceptualists. Even more, I liked the post-minimalists, the conceptualists. I don't like to exclude anyone or anything. For one reason, because I don't really absorb that emotionally. So I can accept things that don't go together. It's fine with me. The only culture I couldn't reach was mine. That was a problem. But I didn't know that was a problem. I constantly am exposed to different things, and somehow I just try to get the best of it. And then I discovered there is something that could be done. So basically, this putting together philosophy and art is something that I experienced, right at that time. The philosophers we were bringing in had no idea what art was. They were not trained that way. I was Americanizing the French philosophers, and they were philosophizing the artists.

DG: There has been a political undertone to Semiotext(e), which has helped define American radicalism. How would you define it?

SL: Well, it's a post-1968 kind of politics: not regretful, but not distrustful. When I came back to Paris, six years after 1968, everybody was disillusioned. Everybody felt it had been a failure. I thought, well, no, I don't think it was a failure. I think I'm up for it, that's closer to what I would like. So when I got a chance to re-create it, I re-created it. But it's a different 1968 than in France. A lot of things that I liked in Deleuze, Guattari, Baudrillard, had to do with that. I don't exclude people: I am not like Breton, the surrealists, or even the situationists. I realized that most people who are engaged in politics from the intellectual world do not take risks. I like people who take risks. I love risk, unfortunately. I cannot live without a certain amount of risk. So I liked thinkers who were giving me that sense of politics.

DG: You were very engaged with downtown nightlife. Can you tell me about that?

SL: It was strangers in the night. People I met would be strangers, and I would get to know them. Like foreigners—the "foreign agent" series, which we created with Semiotext(e). A "foreign agent" is the administrative phrase for a "spy." And those spies are the people I wanted to be with. It was the person I was. I wanted to have a sort of covert action. Even parties were part of that—a covert action to the intellectual world. I wanted to create a special America. New York, such as it was at the time, I totally adhered to. Schizo-Culture, for me, equals New York. That's it. That's what I was thinking: New York is a place, with Columbia, the academe, the artists, Harlem, music, dance, art, there was so much to take in and bring somewhere else. That's what I did. The fact that I was a stranger to all was very helpful. I had no prior connection. People I met, I met them, not because they were part of this or that, but just because I liked their work or I liked them. It was more pragmatic, and that's why I felt I was more American than the Americans, because the Americans were not pragmatic enough.

NIETZSCHE—CAGE

SL: I'm listening. Do you want to speak in French or English?

DG: We could do it in French this time.

SL: Maybe I'll put on...

DG: Your own recorder.

SL: Yes!

DG: It seemed to me, in our last interview, that you set forth John Cage's connection to philosophy, to Nietzsche. This correlation seemed, in a way, to sum up Semiotext(e). What do you think of that?

SL: It's the whole thing about the Cage/French Theory connection. First of all, there's that pretty fabulous story of the lost conversations.

It all started in France—that's the paradox. The inspiration for Semiotext(e) came from France and from French, since Belfond published that book called *For the Birds* in 1976. And *For the Birds* has a whole story to it, because it was the French musicologist and philosopher Daniel Charles who had done some interviews with Cage. But Daniel Charles lost the originals. And so the only thing left was the translations he had done.

The translations didn't have an original they could refer back to: it was a book without an original. To make a book out of the conversations, Daniel Charles had to try to remember certain passages that didn't exist anymore. So he reconstituted the book, like an archeologist. They published it with Belfond where it had pride of place for a few years.

When they gave the texts to Cage, he said, "Yes, it's interesting, but it isn't necessarily me." And he added, "We'll put different colors, inscriptions in a certain style will indicate that I remember having said these words, and the rest are a version of what might have been there in the beginning." When he saw the result, after quite a few drafts, he said, "In the end, why don't we make one book out of it? A single book, with a single style. I'll know when it's me. I'll recognize myself when it's me. The readers don't have to know. I really like this translation."

That's how it happened. I thought I'd read the book in 1975, but it was actually published in 1976. I'd already met Cage then. I thought it was the book that brought me to Cage, but in fact it was Cage that brought me to the book. No one knew about the book in the United States. So I said, "Hey! Cage will be the first Semiotext(e) book!" I had the text translated by one of my assistants at Columbia and I wanted to publish it, but Semiotext(e) didn't exist as a collection of books yet. We had done a few issues of *Semiotext(e)*, like this one, that was done in 1978 with a text by Cage and another by a dancer called Kenneth King, a "Cagian." The issue and the book were two separate things, but they both point to the idea that French Theory was born in France, not in the United States.

What happened is that I had had the book translated, but Americans were not that interested. And so I contacted an English editor, Marion Boyars, because she was publishing texts that were somehow transgressive, Artaud, etc.

I had left the book with the translator, I didn't follow up carefully, and what happened is that Marion Boyars published the book, which was supposed to be a co-production with Semiotext(e), but the name of Semiotext(e) was written in minuscule letters. To make it acceptable, she gave the translator the possibility of writing the introduction. It was one of those deals. And I wasn't very pleased about it.

But it taught me something that had nothing to do with Cage. It taught me about the notion of a group. I have always worked in a group. As we have discussed, I have always done everything in a group up to now, acting as a mediator between a number of people with the idea that it is not so much the individual people that count but what the collective can produce. The collective was really what I had in mind constantly. And it always happened, I always managed to have people around, and when there are people around, then the project is being born. And that's exactly what happened with Cage. But this time with Cage, the connection was deeper than what the French thought and what Cage himself thought.

There was a deeper connection between them than just putting people together as we did during the Schizo-Culture event. It was something of a continuity, even when Cage and Daniel Charles were trying to produce the book. It was already like a collective: the publisher was one entity, and there were several Daniel Charles. Daniel Charles did the composition of the interview, but he also was the one who rewrote some of the book. And there was Cage... Between the two, they already had a group, it was not only two people. Besides, it was written in French and the original was lost.

The book was a warning to me: that what is so important for the Americans is not so much the product, it is the credit.

All through my life, in the States, I always had to be very careful to make sure that the group remained a group and didn't split into little individual things. And that's what I did also with the issue on Schizo-Culture. It was done with twelve artists working with me. But the idea was that I was going against the grain of American culture. American culture controls people by trying to make them strive to be separate and individual, and I was trying basically to do the reverse. And the magazine, for me, was a possibility of going against the grain of the culture in order to introduce something that was foreign to the culture. So, when I read John Cage, I realized that what we had in common is that we are both Nietzschean.

This I didn't expect. Cage was the one who discovered Artaud when he went to Black Mountain College—he is the one who told Allen Ginsberg about Artaud, and that's how Artaud became an influence for the Beats and the Beats had it translated in San Francisco. Cage was already connected to Artaud and to a whole series of networks that existed between French philosophers themselves and between the French and the Americans. When I read it for the first time, I thought I was reading Deleuze and Guattari. The whole idea that "Emotions like taste and memory are too tightly connected to the Self, to the ego. Emotions manifest that we are touched inside ourselves." The whole idea of going, not just against the ego, but also against the famous emotions, the "feelings" Americans have, contradicts the justification of any kind of ego trip, the idea that emotions belong to people. Nietzsche's famed contribution is that the "I" is a fiction. Between Nietzsche, Cage, Deleuze, Guattari, Foucault, we all agree on the idea that emotions are not personal, but that they come from the outside.

It's Deleuze saying, "Life, there is nothing personal about life," which is quite similar to all these ideas that Cage has been playing with, because they were very important for his work, the idea that you have to open the space, you have to control chance in order for chance to be really chance because if you leave things to chance, then you fall back into habits.

Constantly, the idea is that one thing is not one thing; it can only be one thing if it is not opposed to another thing, against binarism. When you compare two objects or two artworks, it is the singularity that disappears, another idea of Deleuze and Guattari, which has to do with the concepts of singularity, event, that have been very important for the French philosophers.

All this was already anticipated in Cage: "I know very well that things interpenetrate one another, but I think they interpenetrate each other more richly and with more complexity when I establish no relation. It is at this moment that they meet, that they compose the number 1. But at the same time they do not obstruct one another, they are themselves. And since each thing is itself, there is a plurality in the number 1."

All this is, of course, so close to and could have been written by French philosophers, and the paradox is that, for the most part, it came from Eastern philosophy for Cage. The French never quite realized how important Eastern philosophy was to the thinkers I was introducing to the States. They themselves were not aware of it. There still is not much writing about the connection between Deleuze, Guattari, the *I Ching* and Buddhist philosophy. When you are in California, you turn towards the East…

In Cage we found the idea of change, which was already in the *I Ching*, and the idea of forgetfulness that you have in Nietzsche, that you have to eliminate whatever prevents you from being singular. You have to eliminate everything, the reactive forces as opposed to the active forces.

As he says: "We strive to lay relations between things, while we lose things, we forget about them, we disfigure them. Zen teaches that we are in reality in a decentred situation in relation to this frame. In this situation, everything is at the center. There is then a plurality of centers, a multiplicity of centers and each are interpenetrations."

This is all the idea that you have in *Anti-Oedipus*, the idea that you don't work with relation, you work with multiplicity. You start with multiplicity. In multiplicity there's a certain form of individuation. Language itself is not important. Language is not separate from anything else. That's what I related to most of the time because I was changing my language.

Actually, the fact that the book was an interview was very important for me, because for a few years I had to conduct interviews because I didn't speak English well enough. Or I didn't know English well enough as a working language. There was a multiplicity of determination, "overdetermination." The fact that for ten years I was doing interviews, because I wanted to have a direct contact with artists and to know them. But also, because it created the material that I could use, and reproduce in the magazine. Also, I started doing things with interviews that tried to push the interview a bit further in a sense. When I did it, I made performances as well. I went to Canada and made a performance with two tape recorders and the two tape recorders were asking me questions and I was asking a question. We were extending the notion, the format of the interview. It also meant that I was never alone. I may be singular, but I'm never alone because we're always establishing contact with people. Relating to them, having them speak, but not writing about them.

How not to write criticism. That has been my concern or critique, actually, of criticism, because even good criticism is always just second hand. We have always wanted to do things first hand and to deal with objects themselves and not with second-hand things, the rehashing of the work. The work is always a philosophy. So you don't have to provide a critique. Of course, that creates a problem for academics. I once went to Poland and explained my position that there should not be any form of criticism. And a philosopher asked me, "What should we do then?"

The reason for my attempts was practical enough or theoretical enough: it was to wonder how you can constantly create multiplicities. How you can always make sure that it is not something that comes from the outside. The goal was that in a way the interview could be a form of creation. That's why I was pushing a bit in that direction. That was one of the reasons I was interested in the Cage book as well—that it had come out first in French.

DG: Then, in the 70s, there was a great American presence in Paris as well…

SL: Reid Hall was the first American school in Paris, and that's why all these people like Lacan, Deleuze, were coming because they had never seen an American speaking before. In 1972, they started doing that. In a way, I was basically rehearsing in France, inviting the multiplicity of voices that you had in theory, Deleuze, Guattari, Foucault, Serge Leclaire, Catherine Clément, Denis Hollier, etc.

Why? As we discussed, I had been away myself for five to six years, during the 60s. My mentors were Barthes, A.D. Coleman, Lefebvre, etc. When I left for Turkey, for Australia, etc., I was totally cut off from the theory scene. When I came back, I created these schools in order to be able to take the classes, to catch up on what was developing at that time, which was totally different from what existed before. You know, that started with Derrida, the attack of Lacan...

The whole scene in France was multiplied out, very antagonistic, very exclusive, and I didn't want to be exclusive. So, I decided to invite a number of teachers who didn't speak to each other in France. I was creating a group out of what was not a group. Because the rivalry was very destructive to creativity in France, as opposed to the States. Rivalry in the States becomes creative because it enhances...

DG: Competition...

SL: Yeah! So, again, the whole cluster of John Cage had to do also with learning how to be an American. You know, we're learning from the inside of the culture at a place it seems the culture wouldn't allow. With a series of disconnected things, I created with people a network that didn't exist before. And that's what we ended up calling French

Theory. French Theory was French because it was half created in France. When it came it was an American creation because it was a connection between things, and it became quickly objectified and fetishized.

DG: Your relation to Lacan is very interesting, and how you sort of wanted to find alternatives to his view. How do you position yourself towards Lacan?

SL: I attended a few seminars. I was actually the first lecturer on Lacan in New York. I gave a class on Lacan. First of all, I was very close to Deleuze and Guattari. So that was it. I read Lacan and Freud. My rage is more against Freud than against Lacan, to say so. But also my relation to psychoanalysis has to do with my past, a lot, because people around me say, "You know, you have a problem. Analysis is great." I tried several times but I couldn't stand it. I went to see a Lacanian in Paris. And that was very interesting, we were at the first session and at the end he said, "The price for the interview is such and such..." And I said, "Okay, you give me a receipt." He said, "Ah! No, no, no. It's against our principles." I said, "I'm sorry, I'm an American. I need a receipt."

So I said okay, enough. You leave psychoanalysis in the hands of people who don't have any control because of the whole idea that you're supposed to release control. People did something entirely different with it. They used it to exert control. So I was very suspicious of it and psychoanalysts were very resistant to that suspicion. Basically, I resisted psychoanalysis because I resisted things that were so very important for me in the past.

The problem I have in my life is that I had to do something without betraying it. I have been involved in a moment of history that was a collective delusion of people. When I felt overwhelmed by it, I thought it wasn't mine. I was there for other reasons. I was there, one of the many witnesses, and some people had it worse than I had, but I didn't think that it was something personal I had to cure.

My relation to Freud and Lacan is of that sort: Lacan also because of the emphasis he puts on language. I was a structuralist. I was a semiotician and part of the reason I created these little seminars in Paris is that I was desperate to try to get rid of linguistics. With the group of semioticians, we were fighting the hegemony of linguistics over the rest—over all the areas of thought. In other words, we aimed to promote semiotics at the expense of linguistics: it means that we already consider language everything that people consider art, that art is a certain semiotic. Art is a certain way of organizing forms of mixed signs, that are not just signs, and of connecting them to other signs, etc., etc.

The group of semiotics was—within semiotics—trying to escape the hegemony of linguistics, and that's why it took me a long time to get rid of structuralism. When I started doing all these seminars in France, I wanted to go beyond linguistics, not only because that was trendy, but also because I realized, "Yes, structuralism is a certain way of relating things." It's not singular things, but the fact that you constantly expel singularity by establishing a relationship. That's what I found with Cage too, that the relation is not important. It is really the possibility of achieving a certain singularity which was materiality at the same time.

I was reading your book of conversations with Pierre Guyotat. I was thinking, Pierre is exactly the reverse of how I am, totally. I also understood Artaud better, from reading the book. Pierre is thoroughly grounded. Grounded in history, grounded in class, grounded in deterioration of the body, which is more than materialistic. Because everything is material, even sperm is material. It is something that you can create with.

The Bible is his Bible. He has this total connection to the 30s and the 40s. We talked about that this afternoon. In other words, he is everything that I'm not. I came to a place where you don't have any identity. You don't have anybody. You don't have anything that belongs to you. All you can do is go from country to country and not get roots anywhere.

Of course all this is plain clichés. The Jews were rootless, etc. I couldn't help it. But at the same time my relation to philosophy is also a relation to someone who is not a philosopher, and who tries to avoid being a philosopher because philosophy prevents me from existing.

I was turning towards all the philosophers like Cage because he's a philosopher, or Nietzsche of course, because Nietzsche is a pivot, Deleuze, Guattari, Foucault. All these people are philosophers. They manage to have a relation to philosophy that is a relation to material. They're not going to abstract things, but to life.

I was in this kind of strange position where the only place that I could territorialize was philosophy. Philosophy was also something that I wanted to get rid of. One way I found to get rid of it is to export it to the United States.

Interviews
and Politics

DG: I'd like to start this new interview by speaking about your films. You've filmed or recorded many interviews with people, especially with artists. Does it bother you that ninety-nine percent of your archive is unreleased?

SL: No. My films are shown, or not shown, partly by luck, by chance. Chance and friendships. My films have been shown in about fifteen places.

DG: When you were accumulating all these recordings, were you accumulating them to make them public, or for some other reason?

SL: For me, they were frozen time. Time passes, but I caught hold of it. I was stronger than time. I have this image of a film camera panning into a corner, and there are boxes and boxes of recorded interviews. That's a bit what I was doing as well.

DG: How did you choose the people, the communities, that you filmed?

SL: It depends. Each situation was different. For example, there was a French magazine called *Autrement*. *Autrement* did an issue called "New York Electric." They asked me to do the interviews. It was an opportunity. My friend Marion Scemama wanted me to do an interview with David Wojnarowicz, who recently had a show at the Whitney. New York gave a unity to the whole, but things weren't planned.

DG: When people do interviews, it's generally a form of journalism. It seems to me that for you it's different—as we spoke of last time.

SL: I've always done a lot of things at the same time, and very different things too. Sometimes, the films were extensions of something I had started. I told you about that interview where I held a dialogue with a tape recorder. The fewer academic texts I wrote, the more interviews I did. It was a way of accumulating experience and theory. Because all of this, for me, was theoretical.

DG: In what sense was it theoretical?

SL: In the 1970s, I did a lot of things on music and dance, because that's what was most alive in New York at the time. That's what people came to New York for: experimental music, Merce Cunningham's dance. The goal wasn't necessarily to go straight to those people, but each interview was, in a certain way, a facet of the thing that interested me above all, and that was New York. Everything thing I did, up to a certain point—let's say until the mid- or late 80s, before the real-estate boom—was a way of breaking into this place that was a no-man's-land but that was also full of so many promising things: New York. New York gave a unity to all that: whether it was John Cage, William Burroughs, dancers. And then, for example, I had some German friends who wanted to interview me. So I did some interviews to complete some workshops I'd done. You see, it took different forms. There were also some interviews with psychiatrists.

DG: We're back to your relationship to psychiatry, to psychoanalysis. Your interviews are also a form of therapy, both for you and for the people whose analyst you become, in a way.

SL: Art was their psychoanalysis. But the interviews were a way of putting things together that didn't go together. It was as if I had various threads, and I followed them. There was the thread of the interviews and the thread of the videos. There was the thread of the films. I made films for a year because I had a loft and I could invite people to come over and speak at my place. Everything was already set up. I had a friend who did video work. So for a period there was a series of long, very long interviews that often led to films. But then I had to leave the loft, and that source dried up. Still, it's the idea of starting out with one thing and seeing where it will lead you. That's when you start to create a network. It's a series of facets of a world that won't let itself be deciphered otherwise.

DG: You have many facets yourself: professor, publisher, author, interviewer, videographer, human being... What gives them their unity, in your eyes?

SL: It's a little bit like the people in the Wim Wenders film: you never know where you're going. You're going, and that's the point. I'm kind of in the same situation. Something is going to happen, but I don't really know how. For me, interviews are about going towards something that I don't know but that is going to be a revelation for me. In general, when I do an interview, I don't prepare for it. I have a few vague facts that allow me to decipher a zone of intensity, but I don't want to already know what I'm going to get when I do an interview. That's what made it interesting, for me. That was the life of the interview, and a way of producing an event. I really have a kind of knot, a time that resists interpretation. It's also true I did it because I've never wanted to go to analysis. Psychoanalytic language repulses me.

It isn't only the language, it's that the psychoanalyst wants to reveal secrets, and I don't want to give them up, I don't want to reveal them through a framework that levels everything out. Artaud said there's something treasonous about going to analysis. It's like cutting at the root of a certain relationship to art, to the world. I agree with Baudrillard: things are secret because you don't even know what you're going to give. But that's what happens in life. You never completely know how it's going to turn out. Everything I was doing was like placing bricks one on top of the other and making a kind of rickety edifice. Each thing means nothing and at the same time it carries a heap of things. There's always a moment when it cracks apart and there is a revelation of something that you didn't know before.

DG: And the people accepted, just like that, to do the interviews?

SL: Yes. They didn't know me at all. And I even interviewed people who weren't artists. For instance, there was a guy who was completely competitive in everything he did. I was interested in that, because it wasn't New York, but it was America: to always be first in everything, etc. So I did a video with him. I never did anything with it, but that's how it is. It was also a way of understanding New York and getting to know the place. New York belonged to me. I've had periods in my life—especially around the mid-1970s, when I still had a car—I wouldn't sleep, but I'd go make the rounds of my flock. I had places where I'd go until two in the morning, other places after three in the morning. I'd make the trip by car and stop in lit-up places, at night. The whole city was sleeping, and I couldn't understand how people could sleep when there was such a current of love, of sex, of things happening. Even when I left New York for a few months, I would come back afterward and have a look here and there at all the places I used to go to, and see how everything was changing. It was also about meeting people at random, you see? I'd meet people who would take me to their homes. We'd talk. I'd put on a tape recorder. It was a certain way of doing things without ever really defining them. These were things that had to do with art, but also things that had to do with life, which is a form of art. You construct it at each instant.

DG: The question of art and life is absolutely central to you. It's in the authors you studied. But you went looking for modes of life that were extreme…

SL: Yes, of course. I'm not an academic. I didn't want to be one. That's why I used the university to travel. As for the people I studied under at university, Barthes, etc., I didn't consider them academics. I considered them inventors. I was interested in that. But as for the rest, I was an usurper at the university. I wasn't making a career of it. I saw the way they treated me, and they had every reason to treat me the way they did. They were right not to raise my salary. They were right not to promote me. Systematically, I tried to discourage people so that, in a certain way, people would stop expecting anything of me. I remember when I had my kid, she was five or six years old, I had a stroller, and the vice-president of Columbia asked me to be on the *ad hoc* committee. When you're on an *ad hoc*, it's the university's inner sanctum: the important thing isn't what you get done, it's the little community you're creating. You get to rub shoulders with the president: it's the Mecca of university life. Because of Barthes, I'd been invited to Japan for a thesis defense, etc. I said to myself: I don't have a choice. I tried to break the whole thing. It was the day I was supposed to go to the *ad hoc* meeting, and I realized that I was late, that I'd never make it in time. So I called them, and I said I didn't have a baby-sitter. They never called me again. It was clear. I hadn't necessarily provoked it, but with the kind of life I was leading, going to clubs at night, it would have blown up. I remember, one time, I was coming back from the Mudd Club where I'd been up all night, and I got to Columbia at seven-thirty in the morning and realized I didn't have time to stop by my place. And so I still had on a spiked leather jacket. I got there, and I thought, this should be fine. Unfortunately, that day the dean was coming down the Columbia steps. I walked past the statue. The dean saw me and then quickly looked away and walked past. That was it. I'd gone down in flames again. I wanted to go down in flames without wanting to, without bringing things to a head. I didn't want to be fired at all, because then I wouldn't have been able to keep on doing what I was doing. So I always did what was asked of me, but the minimum of what was asked of me. I didn't worry too much about the university. But I'd understood that it wasn't interesting to be a university rebel. It's negative energy, if you spend your time shocking people. But I was using the university, and they very well knew it.

DG: And yet you trained several generations of students who became theoreticians, thinkers...

SL: Yes, but now they're artists, gallery directors, actors, so they didn't really follow a classic university track. And also, teaching was the only thing at the university that interested me. I love teaching, and I love it when I don't really know what's happening. Each class could turn one way or another. Often, when I taught Artaud, I couldn't teach him in a rational way. So I'd smoke marijuana. I'd get to class, and I'd begin speaking Artaud. It wasn't Artaud and it wasn't me, but it was a certain way of accessing something that was outside of the norm. Or else I'd happen to have a problem with a babysitter again, and so I'd come with my kid and do the class while holding her in my arms. When I teach, I'm no different than how I am outside the university. If you get comments, you have to accept it. As you know, every year there's a file where the students evaluate their professors. The put in their grades and their comments. Some of the students would say, "As soon as you walked in the door, this class had a very peculiar atmosphere."

DG: In a good or bad way?

SL: Ah! They knew full well that I was stoned. And I didn't try to hide it either, you see. I wouldn't say anything, but it's easy to tell when people are a little high. My relationship with the students wasn't a master-slave relationship. I wanted to get them to understand that the university was a place where you could train very great scholars, but it wasn't life.

DG: You spent your life in clubs as much as at university.

SL: Until the mid-1980s, when I started seeing my students at the clubs. I never went back. There was a moment in the mid-80s when uptown and downtown mixed together. What was interesting about the clubs is that we had a lot of friends, and even if we couldn't have discussions in the club, because the music was very loud, we'd get together, we'd go out on the curb. It was a way of making a kind of floating community, a place where we'd meet up. Someone would say, "Okay, are you free for two days? We're going to Coney Island to shoot a film." So I'd go. I'd do the lighting.

DG: The notion of a "floating community" is interesting. It seems to run through everything you've done… That's how Semiotext(e) worked.

SL: And how Semiotext(e) still works. For me, community isn't a notion. I lived in a community for eight, nine years. Unlike the Americans, I'm not competitive at all. It's the opposite—I like it when people contribute in their own ways. To be able to do things like that in the United States, you have to have a sensibility like mine: I liked work that was done well, so I didn't necessarily let people do whatever they wanted, because we had a goal, a project. "What counts is the project," I'd always say. The person doing it isn't important. I have many criticisms of Zionism now, but the movement taught me that when you're given a framework, you can be someone and you can also be everyone. The same way that you would hand over your clothes, which were owned in common. You gave your clothes, and you became socialized. The *Semiotext(e)* issues were a way of creating floating communities, communities that weren't meant to last. With my German friends, for example, or my Italian friends. That was gone by the time the East Village came up in the early 1980s. It was too mediatized, too American, too competitive. In fact, I never loved America. I loved New York—I was madly in love with New York. But what interests me about America is the great plateaus of Utah or of Arizona. Every year, as soon as I finished my classes, I'd leave. I'd catch a plane, I'd rent a car, and I'd spend a month without speaking to a single person, because New York was so intense for me: you can't sustain that. I remember sometimes I used to go to Jamaica every three weeks because I couldn't hold out any longer in New York. There was such an intense life there, and, after, all that's what New York gave me—and what I gave to New York in return, differently. It was a "potlatch."

DG: How did your relationships with figures who, at the time, were considered marginal come about? I mean the figures whose modes of life and sexualities didn't fit the old norms.

SL: That came from several directions. First of all, there was Deleuze's text on *Venus in Furs* that had opened my mind to those things a little, because I didn't know a thing about them. Just as I didn't know a thing about American art. My relationships with those figures came to me through the gay community: even though I'm not gay, I went to gay parties all the time. I'd get there two days early, have a look around, take off my clothes. People would take me to where there were masquerade balls. We'd go get dressed up. Gay people were a lot more fun than the people who had very particular, very individual lives. I discovered sadomasochism through the gay community. Sadomasochism goes completely against my nature. I'm not at all a sadomasochist, but it interested me. I'd see advertisements for these practices in *The Village Voice*. They were the very first ones, and they caught my eye. Everything that happened in New York interested me, as a way of venerating New York for the possibilities that New York offered you.

DG: What interested you wasn't the Met's eighteenth-century rooms or the Frick Collection.

SL: No. For example, in my film on two dominatrixes, *Violent Femmes*, there's a moment when they say to me,

"Listen, you brought us to this moment, but this isn't for you, because it isn't your form of desire." So I'd become a kind of anthropologist in the situation. I said, "All right, I'll help you speak among yourselves, but I won't switch places with you." It was a little like that with my Italian or German friends, or with the Black Panthers. I put myself at their disposition, I was available. My life is available, and my way of life is about making myself available, so when something would come up, I'd try to see what might be important in it, and then I'd go for it, I'd find a way to be a part of it.

That's why I'd lug my tape recorder along when I lugged myself around in my car at night. Sometimes I'd meet people at two, three in the morning. They'd say, "Come over to my place, etc…" I'd go to their places. There was an element of danger. I didn't know these people. There were men, there were women, etc… I wondered: "What is it to be gay?" So I came home from some clubs with a man, yes, but I'd go to a certain point, and the rest was him, it wasn't me. And so I'd never force myself to do something. And I'd never force others to do things my way. You see. Why did I do the discussions between the dominatrixes? They were right. They told me: "Take your dick there." It's true. I was there as an anthropologist. It had nothing to do with their desire. And so I tried to find someone else that the dominatrix could speak to as an equal, and I'd tell them, "All right, I've set the scene for you—make the most of it. But I won't appropriate this."

DG: There are moments when you keep a kind of distance, and other moments when you are more involved. How did you negotiate between the two?

SL: It depends on the moments. The moments are different. There were moments in New York when I was a little crazy, a little delirious. I had already broken up with my ex. I had my kid. I was leading a life. I don't experience my emotions: I use the people and situations I encounter, like a lightning bolt, an electric zone. They make me feel things, because my own feelings, my own sensations, are too strong. I can't take a step; my whole body hurls itself into it. And so I've broken myself here and there a certain number of times, because I can't withstand my emotions. That doesn't mean I'm not emotional, but I always go all the way.

DG: That's more or less Chris Kraus's narrative of your relationship in *I Love Dick*.

SL: Yes, Yes, absolutely. One time, I went to Japan with Chris. I'd been invited to speak of Kafka, though I'm not a Kafka scholar at all. There was an assembly of thirty or forty people. It was at the home of a psychiatrist who knew Foucault and Guattari. He would stage-direct his own patients. I started to speak of Kafka in Czechoslovakia. The thought of Kafka was too much, my voice cracked. The psychiatrist said to me, "How awful. The one thing you should never do in Japan is show your emotions." But it happens to me sometimes, here, now, when I speak of the war. It shuts my mind off. So I have to choose things wisely, because it's too strong. At the same time, I always used to reproach myself for not feeling any emotions at all. I used to wonder how to do it. I think of nothing. I don't have my own thought. It's as if I was deprived of myself. So I had to find myself again. I found myself a little bit through all kinds of things I was doing. But I wondered: "How do people do it? Do they think all the time?"

DG: The fact of not having your own thought caused you to be open like a field to everyone.

SL: Yes, you're right.

DG: And how did you manage to write? You still wrote books...

SL: Yes, that means staying at your desk. It's paradoxical, because I love to write, but at the same time it's very difficult for me. It isn't only the question: "What do I have in me? What right do I have to write?" Since I don't have an "I," what comes out isn't mine. It's true that was a major factor. When I'd begin something, I'd tell myself that it didn't belong to me. So I didn't finish a large part of what I did. There's no reason to finish it because everything comes to an end one way or another. I don't need to do things ahead of time.

DG: That's a part of your relationship to Nietzsche's thought as well. For Nietzsche, there is no subject.

SL: Yes, absolutely. Nietzsche is a discovery. But it came very early. That's France, the intellect as I want it to be. It took me time to understand all the things I'm telling you. My relationship to Israel, too: when I realized what I had participated in, it completely gutted me. I was totally torn apart, because it was my childhood. Not only my childhood, but my relationship to Jewishness as well. And then to see that all of this is as if it had never existed, to see that it has been annulled by Israel itself.

DG: What role has Judaism played in what you are now?

SL: Well, Judaism—not in the religious sense—I'd say Judaism is ninety percent of what I am, but people don't know it. I wrote a little article "Étant Donné" [Given] that I sent you. It was the first time I was able to touch on the subject. At the same time, I tell myself that my relationship to Judaism is completely in shambles because I would have had to understand things twenty years earlier than I did. I often do things too late: recently I met some Polish artists. My relationship to Poland—I always told myself I wanted to come back to it. Not because Poland interests me, but because in a certain way it's the place where I died. I met some Polish people in Germany. They invited me to do some theatre, and they showed my films. I spoke with them a little, I asked them, "What do you think about the current situation in Poland?" A woman named Polina answered, "I don't know, Polish people don't really know who they are or what they are." I said, "But one can't accept to see Poland become anti-semitic again." Polina said to me, "Why don't you write a short little text, and we'll read it at the performance?" I wrote a little fragment about the fact that the Poles were exterminated by the Nazis and then became Nazis in turn. It said it was time for them to stop, time for them to shoulder their past and accept what they did, and go further. Polina read it at a theatre. Poland doesn't interest me in itself. It's like Germany: when I finished the issue on Germany, I didn't do any others because I'd put everything I wanted into it, but in a fairly secret way so people wouldn't see it, so people would see what they wanted to see. But I know very well what I wanted from it.

DG: You made Semiotext(e) into a political platform….

SL: The last time we saw each other, you asked me: "But what are your thoughts politically?" I said, "I'm on the left," and that surprised you. But my left isn't the French left: my left never declined. In 1968, like Foucault, I wasn't in France. Revolutionary politics became politics, and politics doesn't interest me beyond that. Even if I know the revolution won't come, it's a beautiful thing all the same. Even if all the presuppositions are in shambles, if the ideologies we latched onto don't exist anymore, there's something that's called the left. My left is ninety-percent

Jewish. I can no longer tolerate that people keep doing what has been done.

DG: You were speaking about theory earlier, and you said that what you were doing was theory. In what sense?

SL: It's a lived theory, so I learn things as I go. My intellectual baggage isn't systematized. In a certain way, I've been able to do all the things I've done precisely because I'm not a philosopher in the traditional sense. Because I always understand half of the things I read. So I'm never invaded by a system. But to write a philosophy book, you have to have a system, and I don't have that. That's why I count on luck. I count on the people I meet or the people who interview me. They make me understand things. I need to be helped along. I'm not a true philosopher. Sometimes that distresses me, but I've been able to open doors for myself through my insufficiencies

DG: What is your relationship to philosophy?

SL: I like philosophy for others. I like it that people are philosophers, that they give me things philosophically. At the same time, I wouldn't really want to be a philosopher. I'd be incapable of it. I wasn't able to put together a system. In fact, that's the reason why I could put Guattari, Baudrillard, Foucault together, because they have their turf, they have their ground. My ground is available—available for whatever people want to do with it. But also, I learn things when I do an interview, when people interview me, it's a way of learning, of reappropriating philosophy. Because I always reflect on things in relation to the people I meet or the things I encounter. Yes. You have to have philosophical baggage, but it shouldn't be too heavy! I like baggage that you can carry along and travel with.

DG: It's a little like Virilio, who wasn't a philosopher by training.

SL: Yes, that's it, yes. Baudrillard wasn't either. They were people who dealt in philosophy and created concepts, the concepts they needed, the concepts they had to have. These concepts weren't necessarily part of a system, but they had their reasons, their reason. For Virilio, there was his relationship to his father, his relationship to death. For Baudrillard, it was his relationship to his own insufficiencies. I have a certain connection to Baudrillard because he's illegitimate, he has philosophy bear his children. Him, he has a system. And it's a system that goes toward death. So it's no use going too fast. Most people feel distress when they read Baudrillard. They say, "How can anyone have such a dead world." But it made me jump for joy. I'm a little like Baudrillard; he's a little like me. That's why it was an encounter. Felix Guattari is the one who sees life or the future like a Trotskyist. A future to build. For Baudrillard, it's a future to deconstruct, to destroy. That's what people can't accept. For me, it seems perfectly normal and vital. I choose the philosophers I need. I don't mean *need* in the sense of cobbling together an article. I mean the philosophers I need in order to live.

DG: At the same time, you've come to represent a form of philosophy, in a certain way.

SL: Yes, but that means I'm unworthy of it at the same time.

DG: What's the nature of philosophy for you—is philosophy a theoretical object?

SL: It's a life-object. When I need something that I can't find elsewhere, I have to go find it in philosophy. Philosophy gives me the keys, and at a certain moment I have to think about these keys, turn them into concepts that aren't necessarily my own. Turning them into concepts allows me to take a leap, forward, backward, sideways. I need a philosophy in order to live.

DG: One last question. What gave you all the passion you had for punk, all the collaborations?

SL: It was a certain way of having nothing to respect. It was the idea that something has been lost in our time. I shook Malcolm McLaren's hand. "No future" doesn't mean there's no future; it means we can't believe in anything anymore.

DG: But do you really think it's possible to *not* believe in anything anymore?

SL: That depends on what "believe" means. There were so many things we believed in that collapsed over the years. The planet collapsed. That's what "no future" was: we constantly produce death. A "future" would mean being in control of what's to come, but we aren't in control. It's like Baudrillard: he turns that into a cause for jubilation; you don't cry about it. That's the seed of life. That's punk.

Anatomy
of Subversion

DG: In this series of conversations on subversion, I wanted to ask you, Sylvère, about the space between subversion and transgression. Which side are you on?

SL: I would be on either side. It's a matter of knowing exactly what is the meaning, the value, and the extent of the terms that we use. In other words, in order to talk about transgression or subversion, especially transgression, we have to understand that there's a whole history of it. And it's not just history. The context varies enormously. What it means for a certain culture at a certain time is extremely different from what it means at other times.

For instance, I would say it's very difficult to be transgressive now. If there is an invention to be made in the art world, maybe try to be transgressive in a way that is not just verbal, verbose. Really, what could be transgressive? Is it possible to be transgressive? I'm not so sure.

At Columbia, one of my specialties was the writers of the 30s and 40s. They were very much into classical art, by the way. Simone Weil was a great specialist of Greek, etc. Artaud was a self-taught genius. He knew everything and wrote about some Roman history with precision.

Of course, Bataille. I was the first one to introduce Bataille in this country. We made an issue of *Semiotext(e)*. Then I decided that we were not going to publish it. Maybe that would be a question: why did I think, maybe wrongly at the time, that we had to go to the forefront?

Bataille, in a way, was taking us back. He was taking us back because he was trying to go forward in his own time. Who is Bataille? Like Stalin and Hitler, Bataille wanted to be a priest, the same as Artaud.

We forget, in our culture, how prevalent and important religion was, let's say, until the end of the nineteenth century. It was a catastrophe for a lot of people who were deeply religious, not just superficially, but really into the history of religion, into the practices, etc., who felt totally deprived in the period between the two world wars.

The first war was like a hecatomb. In a sense, it marked a new era. This new era didn't rely on God so much. They were depraved. Like Baudrillard said, "What do you do after the orgy?" They came after the orgy.

The First World War, where 20 million people were killed, was not exactly a very gentle time. We forget that those who invented mass-scale death were not just the Nazis. It happened before with the development of modern technology which, of course, is what Hitler connected with weapons and the invention of new tools for extermination.

I'm interested in the problem of extermination, of course, and death, but what I discovered were these people, who, in their time, were very transgressive. In our time, they're not, but they were then. That's what I'm saying.

Why were they transgressive? There were movements to expand the scope of religion. The church in France, for instance, was trying to enlist a lot of people because it felt that religion was receding. A lot of Jews were being solicitated to come and return to Israel. At the same time, what transgressive people understood back then is that the problem was not transgression. The problem was the norm.

The problem is that when you set the norm, the rule, you have to know what it means within a certain context. For instance, when Andres Serrano made *Piss Christ*. Well, it was a small scandal, but no one killed him for that. If you do a caricature of Allah, you're done for.

That's transgression. In transgression, death is involved. Just think of Foucault. The first chapter of Foucault is "Discipline and Punish." Beautiful chapter, right? On torture and the punishment of Damiens, the regicide. Damiens tried to kill the sovereign and he was treated accordingly. Why? Because the sovereign comes from God. He's been anointed by God. If you do something against the monarch, you're going to be punished on the same body part that did the act you weren't supposed to do. If someone tried to put his hand on a monarch, then it's his hand that's going to be cut. If it's the ear, then the ear is going to be cut.

Transgression means that your life is at stake. That's what they call transgression. When Bataille got interested in the notion of sacrifice, he saw that in sacrifice, the most important thing is death.

These were French intellectuals. They were trying and doing their best to be contemporary. How can you have a religion without a God? If God is dead, how could you be religious? They tried to be religious without God. That means that they created an event, a whole, existence, life, theory, etc. that allowed them to regulate the production of transgression.

Transgression is not something given. Transgression exists in a society where you can transgress. Bataille invented the idea of community and the idea of sacrifice. He realized that in order to create a sacred without a God, you have to make a sacrifice.

You have to get people together. They tried to do that in the approach to the Second World War. They tried to let loose a number of French intellectual males, and they were going to go to a secret place in the Forêt de Marly. They were going to meet, and they would perform an actual murder.

Bataille was working for the Bibliothèque Nationale. They all came separately to the forest. They had no problem finding someone who was ready to be killed. They had a problem finding someone who was willing to kill. That's why it didn't happen.

The important thing too is not only the sacrifice that they had in mind, but that, when a sacrifice occurs, it can only create the sacred if people identify with the victim. The whole purpose of it, widespread throughout the 30s and 40s, is to try to create a bond between people.

Society is falling apart. Why? Part of that has to do with technology again. All these peasants who were encouraged to come to the cities became a mess. How do you deal with a massive mess? It cannot be bound together unless people like Hitler, etc., take care of it. Or Trump.

This is not very easy. I would even say further: it is not just that you identify with the victim of the sacrifice, but you identify with a wound. It is not a personal problem. The main question that transgression involved was: without a God that sets everyone into their places, it's chaos. It's anarchy.

The intellectuals of Bataille's time were willing to be anarchists, but religious anarchists, and they were. I was the first writer that dealt with this transgression. That's why, precisely, I didn't go on publishing Bataille. If we had published Bataille, we would have made millions now. It's such a great academic industry. Dissertations have been born every day on Bataillian categories, etc., which doesn't change anyone's life. What I liked about these people is that they put their life on the line, or they wanted to. Why were they willing to do that? Because they were aware that if they didn't do it, someone else was going to do it for them. They had been around since the 1930s.

Bataille wrote a piece in 1933 called the "Psychological Structure of Fascism." It didn't wait for Trump. They knew that there was what they called a "psychology," a certain mechanism by which fascism is produced: it's a coproduction with the rest of society. It doesn't happen by itself. He was very interested in that.

Artaud published "The Theater and the Plague" in January 1933. The plague: we've heard of the Black Plague, not that Artaud meant the fascists. He was a bit on the fascist side, like most of these people. They were on the fascist side because they had been put in a mine, which was society.

In order to know exactly what's happening in society, you have to be able to fit in so that you can be an extreme leftist and an extreme rightist. They touch each other. That's what Artaud was trying to say. The plague is here. The plague is coming. What do you do to stop the plague?

He talked about the plague. He was invited, which is funny in itself, to talk at the Sorbonne. Imagine now Artaud at the Sorbonne. Of course, he couldn't talk about the plague. He had to become the plague. He decided that he was going to be the baboon that had grown in his imagination, but it crawled between the rows of seats, among the audience. People didn't know what to do with it. He was trying to create a sacrifice and to create a bond between these people.

Some of them laughed. Others left. When there was no one left, except Anaïs Nin who gave us a report on that, Artaud turned and said, "Let's have some coffee." He dusted himself off and he said, "You know, these people don't know that they are dead already."

Artaud was right. 50 million were dead already, virtually, in what was happening outside. He didn't know how to pin it down to fascism. He was so attuned to it as an artist. All of them were so attuned to it that they could speak their own mind or write their own text. It has an immediate relevance.

They were real intellectuals because they never accepted to only talk. There was action behind. That attracted me to them. I come from a culture where death is very important, of course, as it is in the whole of Europe. I wanted to know, exactly, what creates that?

That's where I had a problem with Marxists, not because of Marx. Marx is like everyone else, but people thought that it was enough to analyze fascism in order to understand what fascism is. To understand what fascism is, you have to know what emotions are, and effects. How do you move the crowd? Who moves the crowd, and what, and when, for what purpose?

It's no wonder that in the beginning of the twentieh century you have people like Gustave Le Bon who wrote *The Crowd: A Study of the Popular Mind*, which was read by Hitler, by most people. You had millions of people who came from their little villages where there was the teacher and the priest. They were fighting among themselves to see what was most important, the republic or the church.

Industrialists went and took all these millions of people, who had been kept together because they were in little villages, and threw them in a big city where they were opening factories every day. They were ready to oppress and extract everything from all these people who were ignorant for the most part as to what existed in the city.

You had to know what to do with these people, the workers. Finding a solution to the problem of the salaries, the problem of revindications, wasn't enough. You have to do it concretely. The upper classes were overwhelmed, so they invented people like Hitler, like Stalin, like Lenin, I'm afraid. They had to create a context where these masses were going to be bound, in a sense.

Simone Weil, after she realized that the fascists had won and that was it, everyone was going to be killed in Germany and elsewhere... She said, "Okay, I want to enlist in a factory." She didn't know how to work with her hands, she was the most awkward intellectual there is. She said, "Okay, did Stalin, Lenin ever go to a factory?" but no they didn't, they hadn't. She said, "I'm going to enlist in a factory and I'm going to work there for a year, to know what it is to be a worker."

The others were preaching to the workers. She wanted to become a worker, but she realized, after working for one year in a factory, that these were not people. They were slaves. You see that coming from Bataille and the others too. They were coming straight from Greek culture, the free Greek culture with slaves. They just were slaves. That's it. They didn't have a life. What bound these people together wasn't class, because classes were being formed and fighting each other. You had to find a way of bonding people together between various classes, right? That's what was happening. Everyone was looking very concretely for a way in. Not a way out, but a way in.

Transgression was one of the ways, but you can only

transgress if you know what you're transgressing. What are we transgressing? When there is no God, nothing exists that has any sort of power, weight, or value. We were not crying over God. Okay, he's not there, but what do we do after the orgy of God? That, for me, is the problem of transgression.

Transgression is not something current, because we moved away from these kinds of traditions and beliefs, for better or for worse. The same as I said earlier, it depends where you're talking about. If you're Muslim, transgression is something that's very current. Just make a drawing of Allah and you know exactly where you're going to go within two weeks. What is important for the Third World is not important for the Western world.

We don't understand why bombs are being spread everywhere. It's worth detonating a bomb that will take your life if you see it as a sacrifice. They sacrifice their life. They create a sacrifice. They create the sacred. The sacred is alive with them—fortunately for them, but not for us.

Bataille had a team of researchers. They said, "Okay. Let's have all the knowledge we have at our disposal. Let's forget about it. Let's act upon it." They even had a crazier idea. They said, "Okay. What is important is that we have a sacrifice. How do you produce a sacrifice? We have a sacred but how would you produce a sacred? By making a sacrifice."

Bataille was such an extremist. Extremist on the left, extremist on the right, at the same time. He couldn't care less. What he was saying is that maybe the working class is going to be exterminated by the upper classes, because you have the army, you know that, but it's okay. "We like the workers, but if in order to produce a sacred, you have to kill so many workers, that's worth it, because a sacred is what counts."

When there were revolutions, rebellions in some countries, they were all in favor of the working class cutting the throat of the upper class. What they were doing was not something that was politically marked. They were exploring the limits. That's exactly it. They could be transgressive because they created a norm, and that was positive.

I have a lot to say about it, but that's what I think. We have to know what we are talking about. Unfortunately, we talk in universals. We have universal concepts. We can apply them to a discussion on transgression but some of them have no reason to exist among us. People who are researching this have been searching in the wrong direction.

You talked about a Plato exhibition you are working on. But why not Nietzsche? Nietzsche had an entirely new vision of the Greek. I could see the barbarian in mottled color, and all that. He extracted an entire culture that hadn't been deified. Freud's apartment with all these Greek items, that comes from Nietzsche.

DG: Would you be the curator?

SL: I'm too old for that.

DG: Thank you so much.

SL: It would take the rest of my life.

DG: Thank you, Sylvère, for everything. I felt this was your statement. Can I ask you more questions?

SL: Sure.

DG: You talked about transgression and you left out the other side of my equation, which is subversion.

SL: Yes. You're right. That's even worse.

DG: Go ahead.

SL: Subversion, literally, in a dictionary, means undermining the power, the authority etc. of an established system. *Sub* means it comes from below, and that creates a problem. If it comes from below, if you want to subvert, to topple someone who is on top, the one on top really has to be on top.

Then, let's say, if you go back to Foucault, I haven't really exploited everything there was to be done with Damiens, the regicide. If you want to subvert, you have to have a low and you have to have a high.

Subversion means that the two categories are opposed to each other, and striking out at each other. Foucault unearthed the fact and showed that power doesn't exist, doesn't come from the top: power comes from the bottom.

The whole notion of sovereignty has been used in modern times, where it doesn't apply anymore. The problem now is not how to find a rule, but how to be subversive. It's not very easy to be subversive, you have to know what you're doing. The only ones who knew what to do were the fascists. Of course, the Bolsheviks too. I don't want to go into that, it's too complex and too painful in the history of the twentieth century: to see the very religion of humanity turned into a massacre.

To go back to subversion, if your society... if power in your society doesn't come from the top and radiate down through larger networks—as we well know, we are full of networks everywhere—then how can you subvert something that's at the bottom, or something that makes bottom and top irrelevant? Subversion is difficult.

Who understood that? Look at Hitler. Hitler came in as a poor artist, coming from the street, who had no career, but he spoke well. What he was talking about made people enthusiastic.

He was an injection for the people who were just coming out of the First World War, totally dejected and massacred by the upper classes without any remorse whatsoever. The whole of society had been given over to people who were killers.

There are no more levels today. That means that you can't subvert, that subversion becomes impossible. Hitler was a poor man, who went to the top.

When he spoke, he knew exactly how to talk to people who had been destroyed, and exterminated, and impoverished in Germany. He spoke their language, although the rest didn't belong to his language. He knew he had to infuse emotions into people. The Marxists had that but not when they analyzed things—they did not have Hitler's organization. They were dangerous people because they trespassed boundaries, but the boundaries were those given by bourgeois society.

If you start low and rise high, as a person or an institution, then the world is yours. That's what they did. There are people like "our friend" Trump who talks the language of the workers and does everything against them. That's what Hitler did.

He went to see the chief of industry and said, "Well, you're in a mess. I will bring you war. I will allow you to make money again." But then the chief of industry had to give money to the fascists.

These people were strategists, they knew they were really dealing with people who wanted to exist, to resist, who were oppressed, angry, full of emotion. They knew they had to win them over.

That's why Trump is a fascist because he's the lowest of the low, and he's also the highest of the high. Fascism is both. If you take one of them, it's not fascism.

That's the problem with Trump, he's surrounded with neofascists. Real, deliberate, unscrupulous people. They were going to do everything they could in order to oppress people even more, to expel them, etc. That's why Trump is dangerous, very dangerous. Not because he's stupid, he's not that stupid when it comes to giving people their tweets, especially people who seem to be on the verge of a breakdown—the whites, the white males. The Democrats and other people didn't pay attention to them.

In the 80s, the industry shifted. Industrialists said, "Let's go explore the rest of the world. We don't need inefficient factories in the US, we're going to dismantle them and put them outside." They created a problem and did not want to deal with it.

The problem is that there is a class here that's totally without a voice, without power. It's a problem that didn't die with the fascists of the 30s and 40s. It didn't die with Hitler, the same spring that got people to their feet in the 30s and the 40s and fighting each other is still here. We've been told for a long time that fascism didn't have a chance, especially in America.

Now, suddenly, fascism comes back fresh as a rose. It's at the door and knocking at six o'clock in the morning.

"SCENES AND STAGES":
ON PIERRE GUYOTAT

DG: Sylvère, you're Pierre's publisher in the United States with Semiotext(e), and you've been one of the oldest proponents and admirers of Pierre's work. Pierre told me you first met in 1984, I think when you invited him to New York. Can you tell us about that first encounter, why you invited him to New York and why you were already so interested in his work?

SL: That was connected to my work at Columbia and teaching Artaud, Bataille, etc. Actually, the first time I met Guyotat was not at Columbia. It was at Cerisy-la-Salle, which is a nice little house in Normandy.

I was taking my students there for the duration of *Décade*, the famous conference there. I was there during the famous session about Artaud and Bataille, which was organized by the Tel Quel group. In a sense, after ten days, I realized that there were two camps in Cerisy-la-Salle.

The first was the Tel Quel group, for what it is. Then there was Guyotat. This interested me. I didn't mean to tell you so much about it, but yes, it was very essential that there was some sort of contrast, not to make it into an enmity, between the two camps. Guyotat was, in a way, what Tel Quel was talking about but could never manage to achieve.

Guyotat, Tel Quel, and especially Kristeva and Philippe Sollers, seemed to belong to the same world, but they didn't at all. To explain that, you would have to go into the circle of the French cultural intelligentsia and how it functions in France.

That has a lot to do also with the way Guyotat was received. There were two forms of subjectivity, if you want. Actually, what Guyotat was trying to do from the beginning is get rid of himself, get rid of the *je*, of the I.

Guyotat's position was exactly the opposite of this display of French literary salon culture. What was happening, if you want, is that the Tel Quel group were talking about Artaud and Bataille but were doing everything but Artaud and Bataille. They were illustrating something, but they were not penetrating it.

I remember, for instance, one evening, or one afternoon, where it was a bit rainy at Cerisy-la-Salle, Sollers had taken to table tennis and was challenging everyone. Whenever it was his turn to leave the table to make room for someone else, he refused.

He was the one who had to be the first. He was the one who was telling what the cultural life was supposed to be. That went on throughout their lives. Sollers was the antinomy of Guyotat.

DG: What was Pierre doing?

SL: What was Pierre doing? Pierre, we both looked at each other and we laughed. What Sollers was trying to do, he had already done, ten thousand times. It was so glaring. I didn't know anything about Guyotat at the time. I suddenly realized that this was Artaud and Bataille, there present, not as a character.

They were on such different levels. One was talking about transgression etc. The other one was embodying it.

DG: What do you mean when you say Pierre embodied transgression?

SL: I was surprised also when I met Guyotat in person that he seemed to be in a different world. Everyone else was placed in a definite order, but he wasn't. The French cultural landscape was very well defined, but he was not exactly anywhere. He also had some sort of attitude. He was self-sufficient, a bit proud of what he did.

At the same time, he didn't put himself at the center as Sollers did. Of the two, he was the one who was closer to Artaud and Bataille, and that's what I was talking about in our conversation about subversion last year.

Subversion is simple in the sense that it means toppling all the values. The example that you could take, which is here permanently on the screen, is our President Trump. Our President is an idiot, but he is a real idiot. He is an embodiment of an idiot.

On one hand you had the Sollers gang and on the other hand you had the Guyotat gang, Guyotat by himself. He was a group by himself.

DG: As you became friends how did you follow Pierre's evolution?

SL: At that point the evolution was still only taking place in France. It was totally secret, sacred too.

DG: Sacred and secret?

SL: Yes. It took a very long time for Guyotat to be acknowledged and to be read. He was not what he is considered now, someone who had notoriety. It's only very recently that he had people who were admiring his work and trying to see exactly how it works.

Last time we were talking about subversion. Subversion is what happens when there is no more order. I thought of Artaud. There is a text that people don't often read which is "Heliogabalus." Heliogabalus is a king, the emperor from Syria, Asia, the Middle East. He was offered to become an emperor of Rome, and he came by foot with all the retinue that was going to have the power in Rome. He went towards Rome showing his ass, and everyone around him was toppled. It was the subversion of all the values, the subversion of the law.

Not only that, but all the values that he was supposed to adhere to, he started destroying them systematically. He was surrounded by guards, but the guards were fucking each other. Gays were in the procession. He was toppling all values.

DG: Do you think Pierre is Heliogabalus?

SL: I never asked him, but very early on I was talking to him about Artaud and, unless I'm mistaken, I don't think he was so interested in him back then.

Of course, what attracted me to Guyotat was not the fact that he was imitating, or being inspired by something, but there is something in his sensibility that appealed to me and appealed to him, of course.

DG: Pierre embodied and embodies a sort of avant-garde art, and that's something you were, and are, extremely interested in. That such a thing as avant-garde writing would exist, and that it would be here.

SL: Right. In France?

DG: Everywhere.

SL: In France, art disappeared for twenty years, so Guyotat couldn't really find any inspiration there. After New York took over the artistic power, the French settled in New York and that's it. It was the end of art in France for about twenty years.

It was not obvious that one could find a model of any kind. What interested me is the fact that he wasn't really inspired by Artaud, and that's why I said that he got to Artaud pretty late. What interested me in Artaud was the fact that he was destroying every value that was prevalent in the West.

People don't talk so much about Rimbaud, etc., but what he was doing was what Guyotat was trying to do. He was destroying himself like Heliogabalus. He was not destroying society, but he was destroying himself in order to be able to destroy it in himself.

I was interested in that, the fact that Guyotat realized that in order to write, not to mention to draw—because I didn't know much about his drawings at the time—in order to do what he wanted to do, which was very ambitious, he had to get rid of himself.

He had to destroy himself so that something comes in that he doesn't really know in advance. It is this work on oneself that I was very shocked by, the extremity that he was ready to reach in order to be able to write at all.

There was something again here, very proud, but also very humiliating, as if he had to destroy himself in order to arrive at a point where he would be able to start, and to start writing. This is why I was very touched.

Guyotat understood that the work that he had to do, the questioning of Western values, etc., had to be first implemented within himself. He was not born in a society that made it easy for him, like in the US. He had to somehow recreate a world where values exist. What he inherited was nothing. He had somehow to recreate these values in his own way.

That's why I was talking about transgression. The generation of Artaud, Bataille, and, in a curious way, Guyotat, had to recreate entirely the values that were supposed to exist. To recreate these values, he needed to recreate the values by casting them out from himself. That's the way I understood the effort that he had make—not just an effort, but he had to systematically deregulate incest.

DG: Deregulate incest?

SL: Yes. Artaud, Bataille, Simone Weil, etc., that whole generation of French intellectuals was given over to a world without any value, any god, anything to trust in. All this generation had to recreate it by themselves. For instance, Bataille said, when Artaud died, that he had never met Artaud.

In a sense, this group of writers couldn't do anything other than destroy themselves in order to create values that would be worth inhabiting.

DG: You have followed Pierre's work for forty years now. What do you think of the drawings now that you see them? How do you feel about them and their relation to the work?

SL: Of course, I'm not an art historian. I used to take classes in drawing, but I'm totally unaware of how you make one. I discovered Guyotat's drawing practice very late. What I knew from Guyotat was the textuality he created. In France, everything has to go through text and language to coexist.

DG: What the drawings show us is that his work is also very visual. I also think it's an interesting connection because as Pierre said earlier, and as you were saying, it is important to decipher what comes through language. At the same time, it comes through visions. The drawings are snippets of visions.

SL: Yeah. It's very visual to start with. What is interesting, in fact, is that it's not *visual*. It's *extremely visual*. Like Guyotat or Artaud, etc., this group in which members can only adhere to something if they push it to the extreme. Guyotat joined this group who came ten, twenty years before him.

He didn't have to know about them. He just had to follow his own trajectory until the trajectory took him to something that he didn't know yet but that was going to define his life.

Transgression is impossible in our world. Artaud and all these people were living between two worlds and they were left with nothing of value that they could hang on to.

Transgression can only exist in a society where God, the Law, etc., are in charge. What happened with this group is that they had to confront the annihilation of everything that characterizes the French, their culture, the First World

War. These were people who were born in a panorama of death.

DG: That's also the case with Pierre and the Second World War?

SL: Yes, exactly. He always managed to refer to people in his family who were deported, people who were arrested as resistants, etc. Death was their panorama. I was, of course, very interested in that, coming from the same place, and nearly at the same time, a panorama of death. Death could be something negative.

On the contrary, for them all, death was a way of coming to existence. They were not given value that they could hang on to. Death was what they had to hang on to and to put to work. In other words, what was happening between the two world wars was the fact that the war was everywhere, but the way the war invaded Western life had not been acknowledged.

A certain group had to take into their hands to recreate what had been destroyed. I'm very struck to read that 25 million people were killed during the First World War. That was only the beginning of a much bigger charnel house, which was the Second World War.

All these people were people who were coming from the church, whether they were Christian or not, but they were turning towards people and towards practices that could bring them to life again.

Artaud was fascinated by that. He knew that he was already dead and because he was dead, he was capable of talking about it. Not just to talk about it, but to enact it. You can put that in terms of God, etc. They were not subjected to abstraction.

Everything they did, everything they wrote, everything had to do with death. It came from the panorama of death. I find myself so close to Guyotat.

Each of these interviews is from a specific moment: the first was published in English in *Purple Fashion Magazine*, Fall/Winter 2016; the second and third were held privately in English and French at Sylvère's home on February 18, 2017 and February 27, 2018, respectively; the fourth and fifth were held in English at The Box, Los Angeles, first as part of the series "Anatomy of Subversion" (March 1, 2017) and then as part of the Scenes and Stages Talks (February 3, 2019) organized in collaboration with Semiotext(e) on the occasion of Pierre Guyotat and Christoph von Weyhe's exhibition at The Box.

The third conversation, "Interviews and Politics," and the opening of the second conversation, "Nietzsche—Cage," were translated from the French by Peter Behrman de Sinéty.

1st edition

© DIAPHANES,

Zurich-Paris-Berlin 2021

All rights reserved

ISBN 978-3-0358-0365-5

Layout: 2edit, Zurich

Printed in Germany